Truth has Etiquette

notionpress.com

Truth has Etiquette

Ritwick Alok

notionpress.com

Notion Press

Old No. 38, New No. 6

McNichols Road, Chetpet

Chennai - 600 031

First Published by Notion Press 2015

ISBN: 978-93-5206-358-1

Happy journey

Far is the queue of sure
Pray is the flow of here
Flow is call of scar
Goal is the show of star
Slow is the march of chair
Go is the god of goal

Contents

PART I

PART II

Part I

1. Truth Has Etiquette

Two is the truth of etiquette
One is the etiquette of truth
Fair is the limit of four
State is the gravity of attire
Fair is the four of fun
Fair is the fun of four
Wit is the gravity of four
Witness is the gravity of attire
Fair is the four of fire
Flow is the call of free
Fair is the idea of justice
Suffice is the wit of fair

2. Fair

Witness is the rhyme of fair
Share is the great of wit
Fair is the witness of rhyme
Fair is the rhyme of wit
Great is the gravity of fair
Fair is the idea of justice
Notion is the nation of free
Free is the notion of nation
Call is the great of wit
Fair is the flow of call
Pray is the curiosity of fair
Witness is the rhyme of fair

3. Limit

Fair is the limit of man
Friend is the time of management
Enlightened is the man of hour
Attempt is the wit of great
Fate is the limit of test
State is the fate of mate
Meet is the horizon of fair
State is the witness of hour
Honest is the attempt of limit
Test is the rhyme of fair
Feel is the pure of rhythm
Purity is the soul of mind

4. Pure

Fair is the four of your
There is the your of tree
Share is the tour of true
Tour is the pure of pour
Poem is the pure of power
Prayer is the your of here
Share is the sure of say
Fair is the your of pray
Fair is the four of feel
Fire is then four of free
Route is the tour of true
Four is the your of pure

5. Sacrifice

Sacrifice is the dignity of fire
Call is the fair of persist
None is the there of resist
True is the four of limit
Pure is the moment of consist
True is the share of persist
Share is the ray of rhythm
Rhyme is the pure of pray
True is the your of care
There is the four of prayer
True is the your of hour
Resist is the persistence of fair

6. Perseverance

Perseverance is the galore of concentration
Great is the globe of notion
Great is the love of light
Enlightened is the nation of write
Fair is the enigma of substantiate
Placate is the great of create
Create is the fair of fire
Fair is the four of free
State is the rhythm of light
Straight is the heart of right
Stand is the share of sight
Jubilate is the rare of cite

7. Success

Success is the show of happiness
Bliss is the row of access
Ace is the show of success
Face is the how of yes
Race is the show of share
Trace is the low of fear
No is the fear of loss
Show is the success of happiness
Share is the show of happiness
Here is the flow of hear
State is the straight of heart
There is the three of fair

8. Free

Fair is the persistence of four
Fair is the alliteration of four
Fair is the four of fire
Witness is the attempt of attire
Fair is the four of jury
Journey is the one of fair
Fair is the four of fare
Fire is the four of free
Fair is the alliteration of fire
Call is the flow of free
Call is the free of flow
Fair is the fire of free

9. HJ

HJ is the momentum of fire
Witness is the attempt of attire
Pure is the four of figure
True is the alliteration of fire
Witness is the attempt of attire
Assert is the flow of fair
Pure is the pour of poem
Pour is the pure of power
Prayer is the witness of attire
Attire is the witness of pray
Ray is the fair of create
Fair is the four of fate

10. Price

Right is the price of moment.
Moment is the prize of limit.
Right is the feel of express.
Feel is the right of express.
Great is the moment of fate.
Witness is the great of gate.
Wit is the best of hour.
Gate is the wit of fire.
Witness is the moment of wit.
Beautiful is the detachment of great.
Greet is the gate of detachment.
Go is the god of goal.

11. Synergy

Synergy is the beat of coherence.
Energy is the feat of reverence.
Right is the state of stance.
Prayer is the parade of glance.
True is the route of dance.
Stance is the celebration of romance.
Intuit is the dance of chance
Happening is the happy of stance.
Happy is the journey of soul.
Read is the journey of rhythm.
Friend is the state of dear.
Real is the journey of happy.

12. Determination

Determination is the fire of goal.
Fair is the four of galore.
True is the depict of hour.
State is the heart of hear.
See is the synergy of share.
Flow is the moment of fair.
Fair is the momentum of fire.
Depict is the time of persist.
Here is the ray of pray.
Believe is the life of belief.
There is the limit of through.
Fair is the four of fire.

13. Magic

Magic is the mind of music.
State is the stand of logic.
Fair is the state of share.
Admit is the limit of fair.
Pure is the ray of picture.
Ray is the route of adventure.
State is the fair of limit.
Stand is the prayer of write.
Through is the three of tick.
Pour is the pure of pick.
Synergy is the mind of music.
Stand is the share of magic.

14. Witness

Witness is the attempt of attire.
Rare is the share of fire.
Fair is the persistence of fire.
Share is the alliteration of fair.
Share is the synergy of fire.
Pure is the energy of pour.
Fair is the bit of momentum.
Witness is the moment of attire.
Prayer is the dormant of pray.
Fill is the moment of full.
Fail is the myof hour.
Full is the marks of pour.

15. Persistence

Pure is the persistence of fair.
Ray is the heart of share.
Fair is the moment of pray.
Four is the fire of free.
Roar is the heart of true.
State is the straight of hear.
Fair is the loss of fear.
Witness is the attempt of attire.
Free is the moment of read.
Fire is the momentum of fair.
Prayer is the pay of persist.
Rare is the ray of assist.

16. True

True is the moment of happy.
Self is the sea of love.
Soul is the scent of love.
State is the persistence of heart.
Dance is the reverence of soul.
Romance is the one of true.
Fai is the moment of happy.
Dance is the journey of happy.
Happy is the journey of celebrate.
Elate is the real of write.
State is the state of start.
Goal is the show of star.

17. Beat

State is the heart of beat.
Share is the hear of bit.
Fair is the fear of feat.
Excess is the good of great
Beat is the bit of great.
Bit is the beat of great.
Fair is the treat of tale.
State is the feat of tell.
Date is the tear of write.
Read is the heart of real.
State is the feat of fair.
Right is the pray of prayer.

18. Enigma

Fair is the enigma of fire
Believe is the nature of fair.
Persist is the galore of here.
Depict is the truth of fair.
Real is the hear of great.
Lay is the ray of pay.
Share is the sure of say.
Prayer is the your of ray.
Play is the fair of pray.
Day is the sure of say.
State is the start of ray.
Fair is the persistence of fair.

19. Wit

Smart is the share of wit.
Straight is the heart of hear.
Four is the create of fair.
Fair is the limit of four.
Share is the strict of your.
Fair is the pure of four.
Rare is the your of roar.
Player is the pour of pray
Fair is the player of pay.
State is the share of write.
Bit is the fair of fight.
Cite is the share of delight.

20. Ethics

Ethics is the pen of neutral.
Pain is the state of soul.
Ray is the elate of great.
Parade is the red of red.
Dear is the read of dare.
Real is the lead of dare.
Poem is the pay of pray.
Prayer is the sway of way.
Will is the fair of far.
Fair is the depict of flow.
Fair is the call of flow.
Flow is the slow of show.

21. Momentum

Momentum is the poem of moment.
Rhythm is the ray of persist.
Fair is the moment of assist.
Fire is the four of state.
Persist is the truth of four.
Figure is the state of your.
Your is the state of celebrate.
Rhythm is the dedication of journey.
Moment is the journey of rhythm
Pray is the pay of play.
State is the say of share.

22. Syndrome

Syndrome is the galore of persistence.
Fair is the witness of attire.
True is the four of fair.
Fair is the galore of fire.
Way is the equal of role.
Share is the pal of love.
Fair is the tall of instance.
Share is the fall of flow.
Fair is the four of perseverance.
Stance is the your of dance.
Stance is the sure of romance.
Create is the read of celebrate.

23. Moment

Fair is the wit of witness.
Just is the fair of moment.
Fair is the fit of fate.
Just is the fair of state.
Fair is the right of create.
Just is the fair of write.
Fair is the metaphor of simile.
Just is the fair of style.
Fair is the win of state.
Just is the fair of moment.
Fair is the four of moment.
Just is the fair of one.

24. Gravity

Fair is the moment of gravity.
Pray is the gravity of moment.
Confident is the gravity of achieve.
Prayer is the achievement of moment.
State is the witness of share.
Ray is the confession of pray.
Create is the fair of four.
State is the fair of fire.
Pay is the prayer of moment.
Play is the power of stand.
Dare is the dream of read.
Dream is the moment of read.

25. Time

Time is the best of panacea.
State is the great of ray.
Great is the master of man.
Management is the cure of one.
Rhythm is the supreme of ray.
Great is the prime of pray.
State is the right of cure.
Future is the bright of secure.
Real is the hour of rhyme.
Play is the rhythm of supreme.

26. Mission

Mission is the true of fair.
Mind is the free of fear.
Well is the state of fare.
Will is the best of four.
Fill is the full of fair.
Find is the free of fear.
Fuel is the state of fare.
Fill is the full of four.
State is the true of hour.
Stand is the free of honor.
Straight is the state of share.
Sail is the best of sure.

27. Bit

Bit is the honest of attempt.
Feat is the write of one.
Seat is the state of show.
Fate is the great of tale.
Tell is the fire of feel.
Spell is the inspiration of full.
Great is the journey of happy.
Happy is the journey of good.
Great is the state of cheer.
Bet is the rhythm of fair.
Fair is the rhyme of fame.
Free is the state of fair.

28. Love

Beautiful is the love of drama.
Life is the drama of live.
Beautiful is the life of live.
Fair is the love of beautiful.
Fill is the full of life.
Live is the full of life.
Fail is the my of life.
Truth is the beauty of live.
Fill is the life of love.
Leave is the love of life.
Call is the fair of life.
Fair is the fire of four.

29. Gate

Gate is the moment of gravity.
Stake is the purity of fair.
Feel is the fun of full.
Create is the hour of real.
Share is the moment of map.
Trace is the hour of galore.
Great is the goal of good.
Simple is the test of management.
Management is the state of simplify.
Stake is the great of art.
Witness is the gravity of art.
Belief is the confident of part.

30. Great

Great is the fire of qualify.
Secular is the fire of witness.
Prayer is the ray of rhyme.
State is the fire of rhythm.
Feat is the time of energy.
Fair is the feat of fate.
Great is the belief of state.
Strict is the reprise of real.
Pay is the ray of pray.
Pay is the ray of play.
State is the moment of fair.
Four is the fair of fire.

31. Control

Control is the dignity of fire.
State is the moment of happiness.
Fair is the loss of fear.
Witness is the attempt of attire.
Ray is the control of cheer.
Moment is the journey of celebrate.
Witness is the world of wit.
Fate is the gate of feat.
Fair is the attempt of attire.
Four is the four of four.
Fair is the four of four.
Four is the four of fair.

32. Attempt

Brave is the fire of attempt.
Save is the nobel of noble.
Love is the thrive of live.
Poem is the wit of access.
Fair is the fire of four.
Call is the flow of free.
Fate is the state of write.
Wit is the attempt of attire.
Ray is the pray of fair.
Feel is the low of flow.
Fair is the law of love.
Rule is the lay of pray.

33. Earth

State is the heart of earth.
Fair is the witness of wit.
Poem is the wit of honor.
Fair is the four of hour.
Write is the tie of create.
Curious is the age of courage.
Pious is the page of yes.
Fan is the page of fun.
Gate is the attempt of attire.
Management is the rhythm of simple.
Wit is the fire of pure.
Persist is the fare of great.

34. Happy

Create is the act of pie.
Pay is the say of great.
Admit is the need of rhythm.
Four is the limit of rhyme.
Fair is the goal of one.
Go is the one of good.
Goal is the one of proud.
Good is the great of one.
Great is the one of god.
Go is the god of goal.
Goal is the soul of one.
Happy is the journey of one.

35. Fate

Fate is the feat of great.
State is the tale of elate.
Say is the hear of tell.
Lay is the fear of fair.
Play is the prayer of pray.
Silent is the administration of love.
Silent is the administration of enthrall.
Silent is the administration of surprise.
Sail is the less of sale.
Fair is the admit of limit.
Wit is the three of through.
Fair is the four of free.

36. Grit

Fair is the grit of wit.
Fair is the inspiration of dedicate.
Fair is the gravity of moment.
Admit is the sanctity of limit.
Fit is the feat of fate.
Beat is the bit of better.
State is the share of persist.
Real is the admit of hour.
Sorry is the limit of secular.
Fair is the pure of your.
Bit is the pure of your.
Bit is the your of pure.

37. Equal

Equal is the fate of fair.
Fare is the tell of try.
Pure is the witness of wit.
Sure is the write of create.
Pay is the pray of play.
Pay is the play of power.
Empower is the your of hour.
Happy is the journey of your.
Why is the world of one.
Journey is the one of one.
Wit is the fair of fire.
Pray is the one of one.

38. One

Wit is the gravity of hour.
Share is the limit of moment.
Fair is the fire of hour.
State is the moment of hour.
Ray is the depict of hour.
Pure is the four of fair.
Pure is the four of hour.
Pour is the pure of hour.
Honour is the hour of hour.
Hour is the one of hour.
Pour is the one of poem.
Pure is the 1 of poem.

39. Belief

Belief is the god of action.
Call is the goal of go.
Flow is the four of show.
Feel is the fill of full.
Get is the act of right.
State is the moment of fit.
State is the right of write.
Write is the right of write.
Fair is the enigma of four.
Wait is the wit of witness.
Fate is the state of feat.
Feel is the full of marks.

40. World

Wit is the world of limit.
Fair is the limit of moment.
Witness is the attempt of attire.
Goal is the one of pure.
Give is the full of marks.
Get is the marks of full.
State is the heart of hear.
Share is the light of here.
Straight is the sight of vision.
State is the post of pose.
Show is the post of pass.
Shows are the stop of shape.

41. Spirituality

Sweet is the sweat of spirituality.
Tweet is the wait of modernity.
Wet is the wait of intensity.
State is the best of state.
Fate is the feat of fair.
Pray is the fit of limit.
Fit is the limit of fair.
Feat is the fit of fate.
Believe is the best of belief.
Life is the fest of feel.
State is the wait of fair.
Witness is the attempt of attire.

42. Beautiful

Confident is the dance of beautiful.
Scent is the love of see.
Sea is the life of live.
Such is the romance of truth.
Fair is the rhyme of heart.
Heart is the earth of part.
Create is the fair of act.
State is the fair of four.
Write is the fate of fair.
Fare is the heart of fair.
Wit is the witness of fair.
Witness is the wit of free.

43. Time

Nothing is the better of time.
Time is the best of me.
Fair is the wit of hour.
State is the rhyme of bit.
Fair is the bit of drama.
Fair is the dream of wit.
Fair is the fit of four.
Fair is the feat of four.
State is the fit of four.
State is the fate of fare.
Fare is the feat of four.
Fate is the fit of fair.

44. Weight

Fair is the weight of wit.
Peculiar is the state of fare.
Pure is the happiness of joy.
Fair is the state of wit.
Gate is the go of great.
Honor is the truth of etiquette.
Honor is the etiquette of truth.
Fair is the truth of etiquette.
Hour is the etiquette of truth.
Justice is the truth of etiquette.
Idea is the etiquette of truth.
Fair is the idea of justice.

Part II

45. Glories to the mark...

HAPPY JOURNEY INDIA 2047

Wit is the cry of hour
Bit is the tray of pray
Citing's is the feat of four
Witness is the attempt of tour
Eleventh is the hour of fate
Write is the create of pure
Gravity is the moment of wit
Great is the wit of share
Feat is the moment of four
Happy is the state of journey
Great is the truth of etiquette
Etiquette is the gate of truth
Feat is the best of moment
Gravity is the wit of attire
Great is the wit of moment
Happy is the journey of state

Fair is the idea of justice
Witness is the attempt of attire
Great is the moment of gravity
Witness is the gravity of attire
Fair is the moment of transit
State is the gravity of tour
Fate is the attempt of four
Great is the moment of limit
Integral is the unit of power
State is the unity of diversity
Fate is the free of fear
Witness is the calendar of rhyme
Candid is the talk of time
Flame is the witness of attire
Full is the marks of fame
Rhyme is the pray of now
Won is the heart of here
Fair is the talk of there
Witness is the wit of rhyme
Fair is the wit of hour
Prayer is the pre of prime
Wit is the free of time

Fair is the wit of free
Limit is the four of fire
Brave is the courage of attempt
State is the limit of time
Fair is the management of man
For is the management of man
Fair is the time of free
Wit is the honest of free
Witness is the time of fair
Pray is the play of celebrate
Cheer is the search of Sunday
Celebrate is the moment of seven
Event is the management of one
Fair is the great of state
Moment is the taste of test
Honest is the limit of fair
Fest is the best of attempt
Witness is the gravity of attire
Fair is the moment of fun
Share is the life of live
Four is the moment of life
Best is the surprise of Thursday
Fair is the fate of belief

Witness is the rhyme of attire
Honest is the man of limit
State is the transit of moment
Beautiful is the limit of life
Test is the horizon of fair
Fair is the belief of horizon
Witness is the great of attire
Fair is the love of light
Enlightened is the world of time
Ten is the fair of ten
Fair is the man of century
Equitable is the wit of intellect
Table is the intellect of wit
Stable is the state of mind
Fair is the four of fire
Fair is the four of fair
Fair is the persistence of four
Fair is the four of persist.
State is the quantity of qualify
Quality is the state of quantify
Fair is the persistence of four
State is the journey of persist
Rhythm is the fair of rhyme

Prime is the sure of time
Prime is the time of sure
Flow is the call of persist
Fair is the dignity of fire
Fair is the fire of four
State is the sure of persist
Taste is the test of persist
State is the rhyme of persist
Fair is the determination of persist
Belief is the journey of one.
Unwaiver is the flow of call
Fair is the mind of determine
State is the mind of pure
Power is the test of sure
Beat is the fare of fair
Posit is the positive of victory
State is the fair of goal.
Good is the life of patience
Fair is the belief of ace
State is the rhyme of rhythm
Test is the rhythm of rhyme
Confident is the state of mind

Fair is the begin of here
State is the fair of era
Fate is the fair of near
State is the beat of moment
Belief is the dance of limit
Life is the love of life
C is the eye of your
Prayer is the pour of pure
Stance is the celebration of four
Dance is the your of station
Beat is the rhythm of moment
Feat is the bit of gravity
Bliss is the moment of your
Plead is the grace of four
State is the dance of romance
Witness is the four of three
Wit is the India of 2047.
Attempt is the fire of your.
Witness is the attire of pure.
Sure is the parody of four.
Attempt is the gravity of pure.
Fair is the wit of rhyme.

Save is the rhythm of bit.
Prayer is the intensity of rhyme.
Witness is the honest of attire.
Fair is the pay of pray.
Fair is the gravity of pure.
Feat is the certainty of true.
Prayer is the gravity of secure.
Care is the grit of cure.
Fair is the enigma of four.
Share is the soliloquy of sure.
True is the gravity of access.
Fair is the enigma of attire.
Prayer is the gravity of attire.
Fair is the gravity of attire.
Share is the figure of gravity.
Say is the synergy of figure.
Witness is the gravity of attire.
Prayer is the persistence of fair.
Fair is the attire of persist.
Poem is the wit of attire
Fair is the soliloquy of sure.
Pray is the grit of attire.

Fair is the bit of attire.
Poem is the persistence of grit.
Great is the wit of attire.
Gate is the wit of great.
Fair is the persistence of bit.
Call is the flow of pure.
Four is the attempt of limit.
Fair is the persistence of four.
Witness is the wit of attempt.
Fair is the heart of bit.
Fair is the bit of heart.
Fair is the heart of hear.
Fair is the part of share.
Heart is the part of hear.
Fair is the heart of bit.
Share is the witness of hour.
Brave is the attempt of fair.
Curious is the age of fair
Curious is the age of curiosity
Fair is the witness of rhyme.
Intensity is the wit of hour.
Fair is the twenty of 47.

Stake is the limit of four.
Stale is the mate of cheer.
Four is the fair of prayer.
Wit is the fair of rhyme.
Proclaim is the journey of soul.
Share is the gravity of hour.
Fair is the wit of hour.
Fair is the your of belief.
Fair is the gravity of pour.
Share is the wit of opt.
Fair is the bit of belief.
Belief is the fair of your.
Four is the limit of persist.
Tale is the etiquette of four
Tell is the truth of etiquette.
Fair is the persistence of the.
Fair is the an of the
Persist is the truth of etiquette.
Persist is the wit of great.
Fair is the call of flow.
Witness is the gravity of four.
Fair is the enigma of four.
Call is the fair of flow.

Witness is the rhyme of persistence
Fair is the persistence of belief.
Belief is the fair of rhyme.
Fair is the bit of great.
Attire is the symbol of fire.
Witness is the attempt of attire.
Fair is the fire of 2047.
Fair is the image of belief.
Belief is the fire of image.
Fair is the set of fire.
Witness is the attempt of attire.
Wit is the attempt of rhyme.
Wit is the fair of rhyme.
Parody is the fair of four.
Grit is the gift of four.
Persist is the top of mind.
Fair is the journey of attempt.
Fair is the glory of four.
Blessings is the age of glory.
Glorious is the age of bliss.
Moment is the bliss of four.
Management is the time of 2047.
Fair is the India of 2047.

Wit is the attempt of fair.
Fair is the glory of four.
Admit is the wit of courage.
Belief is the wit of great.
Proclaim is the great of wit.
Same is the witness of here.
Fame is the brim of fair.
Fair is the wit of hour.
Witness is the attempt of hour.
Brave is the moment of fire.
Curious is the age of courage.
Fair is the attempt of persist.
Witness is the joy of pain.
Wit is the paint of fire.
Judge is the mind of state.
Purify is the attempt of limit.
Pray is the great of wit
Fair is the enigma of four.
For is the magic of far.
Play is the four of here.
Pray is the flow of here.
Witness is the attempt of attire.

Flow is the call of scar.
Show is the show of star.
Slow is the march of chair.
Go is the god of goal.
Gate is the gravity of fire.
Great is the gravity of attire.
Witness is the courage of age.
Wit is the four of page.
Cage is the stage of age.
Phase is the tag of attempt.
Witness is the wit of limit.
Brave is the fire of courage.
Courage is the far of brave.
Wit is the fire of age.
Stage is the set of great.
Witness is the fire of moment.
Wait is the flow of here.
Date is the call of flow.
Attempt is the witness of fire.
Witness is the gravity of attire.
Brave is the fate of feel.
Get is the great of wit.

Set is the gate of neat.
Bet is the mate of meet.
State is the taste of success.
Sweet is the attempt of fire.
Witness is the attempt of fire.
Fab is the bit of face.
Shape is the taste of state.
Attempt is the wit of love.
Life is the love of live.
Sure is the belief of happy.
Great is the journey of one.
Note the on of on.
Fair is the ton of far.
Majestic is the curiosity of mystique.
Attempt is the gravity of attire.
Gate is the magic of moment.
Gate is the gravity of great.
Belief is the wit of great.
State is the attempt of attire.
Fair is the moment of free.
Witness is the attempt of attire.
Fair is the attempt of great.
Witness is the great of fire.

Wit is the great of fair.
Fair is the attempt of belief.
Witness is the attempt of attire.
Great is the gravity of pure.
Wit is the fair of attire.
Fair is the patience of persist.
Great is the belief of fair.
Fair is the belief of great.
Heart is the wit of witness.
Hear is the heart of fair.
Fair is the belief of pure.
Belief is the your of fair.
Belief is the wit of fair.
Bit is the heart of fair.
Fair is the love of four.
Fair is the love of your.
Fair is the love of write.
Write is the love of feel.
State is the witness of create.
Fair is the love of create.
Wit is the fire of love.
Fair is the judge of etiquette.
Witness is the truth of wit.

Fair is the four of bit.
Fair is the four of 2047.
Witness is the attire of 2047.
Witness is the attire of fire.
Fair is the four of limit.
Fair is the limit of wit.
Belief is the wit of great.
Great is the fire of wit.
Great is the believe of belief.
Witness is the rhyme of rhythm.
Rhythm is the wit of rhyme.
Rhythm is the cent of scent.
Self is the sea of love.
Soul is the scent of love.
Witness is the rhythm of rhyme.
Fair is the rhyme of wit.
Fit is the feat of wit.
Beat is the wit of great.
Great is the beat of wit.
Bit is the beat of fair.
Fair is the four of far.
Witness is the rhyme of bit.
Beat is the time of management.

Management is the bit of simplify.
Fair is the four of management.
Management is the time of four.
Light is the management of time.
Great is the management of rhyme.
Happy Journey is the journey of happy.
Great is the wit of attire.
Fair is the idea of justice.
Wit is the great of attire.
Fair is the limit of 2047.
State is the wit of pure.
Wit is the pure of fire.
Witness is the attempt of attire.
Fair is the limit of four.
Belief is the four of prayer.
Witness is the attempt of rhyme.
Rhyme is the attempt of four.
Fair is the limit of attire.
Belief is the great of wit.
2047 is the wit of great.
Good is the goal of attempt.
Witness is the attempt of rhyme.

Witness is the attempt of limit.
Witness is the attempt of 2047.
Great is the god of middle.
Great is the god of mother.
Great is the god of INDIA.
Great is the god of 2047.
Great is the goal of good.
Fair is the alliteration of fire.
Persistence is the rhythm of attire.
Pure is the liberation of fire.
Witness is the attempt of attire.
Figure is the four of fair.
Prayer is the rhythm of rhyme.
Ray is the real of share.
Pray is the player of prayer.
Care is the rhythm of fire.
Prayer is the dignity of fire.
Prayer is the witness of attire.
Ray is the rhythm of rhyme.
State is the rhyme of rhythm
Rhythm is the state of rhyme.
Right is the state of write.

Fair is the rhyme of fire.
Fair is the fire of rhythm.
Fair is the fire of four.
Face is the state of share.
State is the fire of face.
Fate is the feat of neat.
State is the sit of face.
State is the seat of fair.
Four is the elate of face.
Honest is the integrity of great
Figure is the attire of fair
Depict is the limit of persist
Inspect is the moment of transit
Fair is the limit of 1947
Great is the wit of 2047
State is the limit of four
Project is the great of nation
Mention is the witness of notion
Brave is the fate of great
Great is the journey of happy
Witness is the attempt of rhyme

46. Full Marks

Rhythm is the dedication of journey.
Curriculum is the symptom of love.
Moment is the journey of rhythm.
Portfolio is the domain of atmosphere.
Rhythm is the domain of atmosphere.
Portfolio is the rhythm of domain.
Segmentation is the therapy of domain.
Section is the love of rhythm.
Design is the curriculum of love.
Rhythm is the part of portfolio.
Synergy is the domain of love.
Curriculum is the atmosphere of syndrome.

47. Happy journey

Man for management time.
Even for even event.
Worry for what.
Jury One! Journey ONE!
HAPPY JOURNEY...